Looking *for* Redbirds

40 Days of Encouragement That We Are Never Alone

A DEVOTIONAL BY
DORI GRASSAU

Looking for Redbirds:
40 Days of Encouragement That We Are Never Alone
By Dori Grassau

Published by SPARK Publications
2116 Crown Centre Drive, Suite 300
Charlotte, NC 28227

Scripture quotations are taken from
The Holy Bible, New International Version
Copyright © 1973,1978,1984 International Bible Society
Used by permission of Zondervan Bible Publishers.

Printed in the United States of America

Printing History
Paperback, June 2018, ISBN# 978-1-943070-45-9

SEL032000 SELF-HELP / Spiritual
REL012020 RELIGION / Christian Life / Devotional

I dedicate this book to my grandmother, Josephine Longo, who loved me just the way I needed to be loved. She always had a calm, peaceful way about her. Because of her, I knew that I was never alone.

Contents

Introduction

"Look at the birds of the air; they do not sow or reap or store
away in barns, and yet your heavenly Father feeds them.
Are you not much more valuable than they?"
– Matthew 6:26 NIV

E ven the birds of the air are not left alone. Our Lord gave us this assurance in the Sermon on the Mount. He feeds them and takes care of all of their needs, so if He does this for the birds of the air, why would we question whether we are alone? We may sometimes feel that we are alone, but the truth is, we are not.

Yet, the feeling of loneliness is a natural struggle that I believe everyone goes through at some point and time in their life. There was a time when I was feeling very discouraged and afraid about many things.

One afternoon I was eating Chinese food and once I finished my meal, I opened the fortune cookie and it said that the color red was going to become very important to me. It made no sense to me so I quickly discarded the fortune. That night I briefly thought about it again and prayed for God to give me a sign that He was with me before drifting off into a deep sleep. I had the most amazing dream. It is hard to explain, but the dream was a quiet, misty, pure white backdrop of snowflakes just floating slowly through the scene of my mind. In slow motion, a red cardinal flew through the mist and when I awoke I felt such a peace in my spirit. I felt like it was the Holy Spirit coming to me in my dream to give me that sense of peace. A knowing, perhaps that everything would be all right.

The next morning the color red was still prevalent in my mind as I got ready then drove to work. I remembered my petition for a sign and thought to myself that maybe I was being silly. Before I could even move onto another thought, at that very moment a bright red cardinal swooped down and flew right above the hood of my moving car. It took my breath away. I knew in an instant that it was God comforting me, telling me that I was not alone. It was my sign.

Every day it seemed like I would spot a red bird nearby. Maybe it was a coincidence, but one day as I approached my neighborhood on my way home from work, a red bird flew right in the middle of the road I was driving on and stood there not budging! Of course at the last moment, he flew away. How many times do we miss seeing the Holy Spirit working in our lives because we are not looking for Him? It could be in the smallest of things, but I believe, there are signs everywhere.

My prayer for you is that when you read this book you will be able to release your burdens, whatever they are, to the One who is always with you; that you may have open eyes and mind to see the Holy Spirit in the midst of your busy life; and that you will receive your very own Red Bird that is especially for you.

He Loves Me;
He Loves Me Not

I remember summer days as a young girl, sitting in the tall grass picking daisies and pulling the petals off one by one. With each petal I would alternate the statement: "He loves me; he loves me not." Then the wind would come along and blow the petals away from my reach.

Most girls dream of finding someone who loves them. We dream of someone who will care for us and protect us. Life doesn't always go as we planned. But I do know that there are seasons for everything. Just as the flowers grow in the spring new and fresh, our hearts at one point were new and fresh as well. Expectations were high, our hearts were pure, and then someone came along and crushed us. They yanked us up by the roots and seemed to kill whatever dreams were in us.

But with each disappointment we must learn to carry on. It's up to us to take those disappointments and turn them into learning experiences. We must take the seeds and replant in new fertile soil that doesn't contain the weeds of bitterness and sorrow. If we don't, then the next people who come along in our lives may be judged incorrectly, and we would miss out on opportunities to love and be loved in genuine ways.

Perhaps we should view each person that comes into our lives like those petals off a flower. They come into our lives for a reason or a season. Maybe it is to show us love just when we need it. Maybe they are here to teach us a lesson about something. Either they stay for a season and then are gone, or they are rooted in our lives so deeply that it wouldn't be the same if they were gone. They impact us. They move us. Whether it is for the good or bad it is up to us to decipher which one they are and then to hold on or let the wind blow them away.

This brings me to a memory I have of when I was newly separated from my husband of thirteen years. It was one of the loneliest times. My life with him was all I had known. I struggled each day to keep myself together and to view life in a new way. I wanted to see the good things in each day, no matter how small they were. I was praying in my car one morning as I was on my way to the coffee shop. I wanted to know if there was anyone that truly loved me.

As I stepped out of my car, I saw something blowing across the parking lot, and it blew right across the top of my foot. I reached down and picked it up off of my foot, and it was a picture of Jesus. My heart was beating so fast. I was in disbelief and awe that the master creator of those daisies I picked so long ago could tell me just when I needed it that HE LOVED ME. I keep that picture on my corkboard at home. It reminds me that I am not alone, and even though life might disappoint us and leave us feeling lonely at times, there is a God that truly loves us.

Love That Transcends Time

Who really knows you? Do your parents know you? Do you have a childhood friend who knows you? When I say know you, I mean do they know your heart and the way you feel and think? Do they know what makes you tick? Do they know how you will react to things and situations? He or she is the one person who knows all about you, even the bad parts, but loves you anyway. A good girlfriend of mine once told me that we could call each other any time day or night and would be there for each other. Such a friend is the one person in your life that you can be "real" with.

My grandmother once told me that I would have many acquaintances in my lifetime but very few friends. She was right. I can count my true friends on one hand.

My grandmother was that person who truly knew me. She always showed me unconditional love. She was a short, but thin, Italian woman with the most beautiful olive skin and long dark hair that she always wore up in a French twist. She had the biggest, sweetest brown eyes that just radiated with love.

She was kind and slow to anger, but she knew what she believed in and what she did not believe in. Her faith was rock solid, and it showed by the way she treated others. Most of all, she had the incredible ability to forgive and let things go.

I grew up in a very tumultuous household and she was the one person I could always count on. She was the only security I had. I knew that I could escape my life when I was at her house. When school would end each year, I would pack up my clothes and stay with her and my grandfather during my summer break. It was a time of peace for me. I felt safe and cared about.

The environment at her house was completely different. I can still remember the way the clean, cool percale sheets felt on my skin as I climbed into bed for the night. The tic-tock of the grandfather clock in her kitchen would lull me to sleep.

At home nobody ever said my name, unless I was in trouble or they needed me to do something. I learned how to become very invisible to stay out of trouble and to avoid any kind of strife. However, when my grandmother spoke to me, I seemed to matter. She was interested in my life and what I wanted to do or who I wanted to become. She would say to me, "Dori Jo, you can do anything you set your mind to." "Dori Jo, I love you." "Dori Jo, don't let anyone else define who you are." To this day, I think there is power when you speak someone's name to them. It exemplifies how important they are to you.

She showed me by example that no matter what happens to us in life, we just have to keep pressing on. It's what sets apart those that fail from those who succeed.

I dreaded the days when the summer time would wind down and I would then have to return home. But with each passing year, I would always leave with more of her love instilled inside of me. So when the bad times came, I could draw upon that strength. During my high school years, a lot of my decisions where based on the question of whether a certain action would let my grandmother down. It kept me straight and out of trouble. I never wanted to disappoint her.

It was very hard to see my grandmother get older. It didn't seem possible that such a beautiful spirit could become so weak and that the hands that once brushed my hair could be riddled with arthritis. It didn't seem possible that the same woman who carried me through so much could forget my name.

I will never forget when I had to move away, and when I returned back to town, I had to go see her in a nursing home. She didn't even look the same. She looked so defeated and disoriented. My heart broke because I knew there was nothing I could do for her. I couldn't change the deterioration of her body or her mind. I couldn't make her eat or give her back her will to live. I wanted her to recognize me and talk to me about things in the past. I wanted her to tell me how proud she was of me. I wanted her to know just how much I loved her. I wanted her to remember how I would tell her every day that I loved her just as much this day as I did any other day. As I held her hand, I kissed her forehead and told her, "Grandma, I love you so much," yet nothing came back to me but an empty stare from her beautiful brown eyes. The silence was deafening to my heart.

I didn't want to leave that room, but I couldn't bear to see her that way. I didn't want to walk away from her down that long hallway to the door that led outside. I knew in my heart of hearts that once I pushed that glass door open to the outside, I would never see her again.

I forced myself not to look back at her, and almost as though in slow motion, as I put my hand on the door to leave, I could hear her small sweet voice calling out to me, "I love you, Dori Jo."

Although our bodies and minds may fail us, I believe that within us lies the greatest gift of all. That gift is love, and it can never fail.

DAY 3

He Just IS

It had been a busy first day of school. With dinner made, all of the paperwork filled out for two children, showers taken, and backpacks prepared for the next day, it was finally time for bed. My twelve year old had finally laid his head on his pillow ready for a good night's rest. With the lights turned off and hugs given, I finally climbed into my own bed, and my mind began worrying about a myriad of problems that were weighing on me.

Moments later, in walks my son who says to me, "Mom, I was wondering: I know that God created us and everything else, but who created God?" How do I answer a question like this? All I could come up with was, "He just IS." There really wasn't any philosophical answer here. I said that I thought maybe there are things in this life He doesn't want us to understand because if we understood everything we wouldn't need God. My son seemed satisfied with the answer and found his way back to bed.

But it left me with a lingering sense that sometimes I tend to over-think my problems instead of just trusting in the One who just IS—the One who scripture says knows the number of hairs on my head and had my days all planned out for me before I was ever born. I go over each thing in my mind that I need to resolve or the things I fear, instead of just laying them down at the feet of the One who just IS.

As I thought of my son and his perfect timing, I closed my eyes and smiled. I was so thankful for all that I did have and the worries of the day seemed to fade away.

I Say Yes

A few years back I had gone to a writing retreat sponsored by Maureen Ryan Griffin at Sunset Inn Bed and Breakfast in Sunset Beach, North Carolina. She had encouraged us to do what's called a "five minute sprint." She gives us a title, and we just write down whatever comes into our minds. There is no editing allowed along the way, and we are not allowed to pause. We just have to write the whole time. You would be amazed at what can come out of your subconscious when doing this.

She gave us three words: I say yes.

Here's what came out on paper:

1. I say yes to accepting myself as God created me.
2. I say yes to being tender hearted for that is how I am wired, no matter what the world says I am to be.
3. I say yes to always working hard and pushing forward no matter how discouraged I may feel.
4. I say yes to the still, small voice inside of me. It's about following my dreams.
5. I say yes I am a good parent.
6. I say yes to going to bed when I am tired.
7. I say yes to taking a walk when I need some exercise.
8. I say yes to setting down the soda and picking up the water!
9. I say yes to messy bedrooms and shoes left on the living room floor. Life is too short to get worked up over nothing.

10. I say yes when my children want me to scratch their backs or watch a kid movie with them.

11. I say yes to anything that might be out of my comfort zone or scary. If I don't, then how will I know what will be gained by doing it?

Saying yes can be a scary thing. It pulls us out of our comfort zones. I think if we stayed in our comfort zones our whole lives, then God could not help us stretch into being better people.

Deuteronomy 31:8 says, "The Lord himself goes before you and will be with you; he will never leave you nor forsake you; do not be afraid; do not be discouraged."

So what is it that YOU say yes to? What is there to be afraid of?

I challenge you to do your own sprint. Pull out your pen and paper and just start! Then tape it up somewhere you will see it every day to remind yourself of everything you can and will say yes to!

DAY 5

To Love Is a Risk

C.S. Lewis said, "To love at all is to be vulnerable. Love anything, and your heart will certainly be wrung and possibly be broken. If you want to make sure of keeping it intact, you must give your heart to no one, not even an animal. Wrap it carefully with hobbies and little luxuries; avoid all entanglements; lock it up safe in the casket or coffin of your selfishness. But in that casket—safe, dark, and motionless, airless—it will change. It will not be broken; it will become unbreakable, impenetrable, and irredeemable. The only place outside of Heaven where you can be perfectly safe from all the dangers of love is Hell."

I think we were all created to love and be loved, but over time we are hurt by others or by the loss of someone we loved, and we begin to build up walls where we tell ourselves things that seem to justify the lack of reaching out to others. By doing this, we obstruct our own abilities to receive love and what could be wonderful if we would only reach out to receive it. Instead of our hands being open, our fists are closed as we say that we don't want to be controlled by anyone ever again. We want to do what we want, when we want to do it, and without having to answer to anyone. We don't ever want to feel the type of pain again that we felt over those losses. We make excuses to ourselves, and they sound good to a point.

We keep ourselves busy with work, projects, friends, technology, but eventually the night comes when we lie in our beds and wonder what would happen if we could just break free of stubbornness and open ourselves up to being loved once again. If only we could allow ourselves to take the risk and love another. Yes, they might disappoint us. Yes, we might disappoint them. But that is life. We are all human and make mistakes. Mother Teresa said, "Love, to be real, must cost! It must hurt. It must empty us of self!" I wish it didn't, but I know it is true.

As I get older, I realize that life is short, and I long for the companionship that I know God wired me to have. He wired me to give my love to someone. He wired me to care and to touch, to kiss and give my heart and kindness to someone who wants it just as much as I do. I know that to love is to risk being hurt once again. My fists aren't as tightly closed as they once were. They are starting to open to the possibility of love and being hurt again and the wild journey they would endure if only someone would put his open hand in mine and take the journey with me.

DAY 6

Courage

"Success is not final. Failure is not fatal.
It is the courage to continue that counts."
– widely attributed to Sir Winston Churchill

I have to admit: the last eight years have been some of the toughest years I have been through. It's been an emotional and financial rollercoaster ride. Quite frankly, I've often thought, "I'm ready to jump off! Undo the harness and let me off this thing, so I can put my feet on solid ground."

We are talking about the death of a loved one, divorce, singleness, financial struggle, teenager "issues," and a myriad of just normal everyday struggles. But somehow I try my best each day to see the good in something, even a little victory. It counts, and it gives me hope to keep carrying on. If I let those feelings of discouragement plague me, then I fail, and somehow the enemy has won. I can't stand that feeling.

Many days I have let fear keep my feet planted in quicksand, forever striving, knowing what I need to do, but somehow letting that fear keep hold of me so that I can't move forward. I feel like I'm not on solid ground. I'm just trudging along, living a life of redundancy. I'm not following the call that I feel God has put on me because I feel afraid. I feel like life always knocks me down just as I get going.

Joyce Meyer has a great acrostic for fear: false evidence appearing real. I love that. We tell ourselves all kinds of things that keep us from God's best for our lives. "I'm not smart enough." "Nobody really loves me." "I can't do this." "My life sucks." "Things will never get better." You know the lines we tell ourselves; we all have them. The problem is that we have to recognize them as they happen and take a hold of them and replace them with God's truths. What does He say about us?

We say: "I can't do this."

He says: "I can do all things through Christ who strengthens me" (Philippians 4:13).

We say: "My life sucks."

He says: "For I know the plans I have for you, plans for good and not for evil, plans to give you a hope and a future" (Jeremiah 29:11).

We say: "I feel so alone."

He says: "I will never leave you or forsake you" (Hebrews 13:5).

I know these things are true. I know I have failed in many things, but those failures do not define who I am as a person. I do get down many days, but I refuse to be out, so I just keep pressing on. Maybe someday soon I will step out of the quick sand and onto the solid ground of His word. I know that I need to believe it with all my heart and to have, as a friend once told me, "crazy faith." It's the kind of faith that gives us the courage to do it even if we are afraid.

I want that. Don't you?

It's the Little Things

It's the little things. You hear people say that. What does that mean to you? I can tell you what it means to me. I think it's what we want to be able to reflect on when our last day comes and to say with no regret, "Those were the things that mattered, and I grabbed hold of them. I lived my life to the fullest. My memories are all I have, and they are good."

I know we all have regrets, but I just don't want to focus on those things any longer. I want to live life to the fullest. When I say this, I don't mean material things because over time those things fade away; they can't bring us what really matters in this life. I know I am a melancholy person in general, but hey it's how I've always been wired. I can have fun and laugh, but matters of the heart matter the most to me!

This is how I want my life to look, and I'm going to be brutally honest here:

- That I loved—I long to have someone in my life to whom I can give my all. I have so much to give.
- That I allowed someone to love me—someone who can surrender his past "bad" experiences and just take me for who I am and to accept my love and care and to treat me with love and kindness.
- That I was able to forgive myself and those who hurt me.
- That I saw God in the little things such as a child's smile, a sunset, a glance at two people embracing, a flower blooming in the middle of a weed patch, an act of kindness, my children's laughter, and more.

- That my children will always know how deeply my love runs for them.
- That my home will be filled with friends, family, laughter, and red wine. I love fall nights spent on the patio with tiki torches lit, sitting around the table with a hot fire burning and great conversation flowing. Nothing better!
- That I kept pressing on even when it felt like the world was against me.
- That I was generous to others even when I didn't have much myself.
- That I never lost my faith in the One who gave me this life. I don't want to waste it on anger and pettiness.

In Luke 12:15 Jesus said, "A man's life does not consist in the abundance of his possessions."

I guess that's true. I've never seen a hearse followed by U-Hauls on the way to a cemetery! So what memories are we making? What will people say about us in the end? Will it be about how we loved others and how they loved us? I hope so.

Pizza Crust
in My Sink

I'm sure you've heard the saying "don't sweat the small stuff." Yet we all do it at some point. But the older I get I am realizing that it is a two-sided coin. There is the negative side of sweating the small stuff, and then there is the positive side of enjoying the small things in life.

We can get all wrapped up in complaining and only seeing the negative things in our lives. Over time, I have found that if I focus on and watch for negative things, then that is exactly what I will see on a regular basis. If I change my way of thinking and seeing things, my viewpoint will become more positive, and things that I let bother me before do not even matter to me any longer.

That brings me to the pizza crust in the sink scenario. I can laugh about it now, but at the time it put our house in a stew of tension that seemed to simmer for days.

It had been a busy weekend day, and I didn't really feel like cooking, so we decided to order pizza and take it easy the rest of the evening. We all enjoyed our pizza and went our separate ways throughout the house to watch TV, relax, or whatever. Someone—we will not mention names—noticed a pizza crust had been left in the sink instead of being rinsed down the disposal.

I happened to be downstairs working on a project, and my wooden art easel was on the table where I was sitting. This person walked past me and stomped up the stairs on a mission to find out exactly who had committed the crime.

I held my breath as I listened to the voices coming from upstairs. The question was met with chuckles because it was thought to be a joke. We were surprised to learn that it indeed was not a joke, and this pizza crust in the sink was a serious breach of kitchen cleaning duty.

Who would have thought? It became extra apparent that it was no laughing matter when the questioner marched back downstairs, grabbed my wooden easel, and broke it in two over their right knee!

I was not expecting that reaction at all, and in a sense, breaking that easel broke a bit of the respect I had left for this person. Why, when life can be so short, are we worried about pizza crust left in the sink?

What is your pizza crust? Is it when your kids leave their shoes all over the house? Is it when they leave the lights on when they leave a room? Is it the fingerprints they leave on the wall? How about when we ask them to wear shoes outside to prevent holes in their socks, but they go out in their socks anyway?

Those things bother me, but not like they used to. I bite my tongue many times. I turn off the light, I wash off the fingerprints, I buy new socks, and I pick up shoes. Or I ask them to do it themselves, and most of the time they say, "Oh, I'm sorry," and they go and do it. No stress. No tension. I choose to pick my battles because I know that before long they will no longer be here and I will long for the days when they were young. For Christmas, my daughter bought me a new easel, and as I opened it we both smiled and hugged. It was a good day, with no pizza crusts in sight.

Broken Dreams

*"The future belongs to those who believe
in the beauty of their dreams."*
– Eleanor Roosevelt

D on't we all grow up with a plan or dreams of what we want our lives to be like? Yet along the way, things don't always go as planned, and our dreams seem to get farther and farther out of reach. We live each day in the monotony of the routine, and somehow joy continues to elude us.

I just don't think we were meant to live this way. I think we were created to live a good life, and that doesn't necessarily always mean in a monetary way. A good life is not completely measured by how much stuff we have or what kind of cars we own, even though those things can give us comfort. How many pairs of shoes we have—now that may pique my interest! But really it's the heart of the matter that matters.

What are your dreams? Are they attainable? Have you ever stopped and really put some thought into what they are, and if so, what you would do to attain them? Are they realistic? Would they bring good to your life and to the lives of others? What's keeping us from following our dreams? I can tell you what stops me: fear. I hate that I sometimes let fear control me. Sometimes I push through the fear and then wonder why I waited so long. There is nothing to fear but fear itself—right?

Maybe it is God who plants the seeds of dreams within our hearts, and it is up to us to nourish those dreams until they are real and alive. So if He is the one who plants the dreams within us, then maybe we should push past the fear because we know that what He wants for us is greater than any fear we can face. Maybe the enemy of that dream wants us to fear so that we can never accomplish what was meant for us, thus rendering us helpless and unsatisfied with our lives. It's just a thought.

I can tell you some broken dreams I had. As a child I wanted a family that was whole and loved each other, but instead I was witness to some things a child should not witness. As a teenager I wanted parents who looked after me and gave me guidance, but they were never around. As an adult I wanted my marriage to work. I loved my husband. I kept a clean house and had dinner on the table each night. And I was the best mom and wife that I knew how to be, but my marriage dissolved. At that point I was done dreaming. I was discouraged and thought dreaming was for fools.

But you know what? As I got farther away from those times in my life, I began to see things in a different light. I saw that when I was young, my grandmother stepped in and took me out of my tumultuous home environment whenever she could and provided a safe haven. I saw that God brought me my best friend, Laurel, who is still a friend to this day. We have known each other for thirty-five years. In her house I experienced what a real family looks like. Her mom gave me guidance when I needed it. When my marriage fell apart, I learned to lean on a God who was there for me more times than I realized. It strengthened my faith because He was all I felt I could lean on at the time.

So over time, I began to dream again. I have little dreams and big dreams, and I know that my plans may not be the ones that ultimately happen. But I try to remember that dreaming is good because it keeps the seeds of hope alive in us and allows our hearts to remain open to whatever comes our way.

Everything Changes

I parked in front of a particular tree each morning as I arrived at work. In the cold of winter, the tree was bare and brittle. It had no leaves, and nothing about it looked appealing or inviting. It offered no comfort or shelter for the birds. I often felt like that tree. Nothing in my life seemed to be going as it should. I felt like so much had been stripped away from me that I had nothing to offer. I couldn't comfort anyone because I myself could not be comforted. I couldn't offer anyone the shelter of my love because I didn't feel taken care of or loved myself. Somehow parking in front of that tree each day gave me some sort of comfort. I could relate to it every time I looked at it. I would actually get mad if someone parked in "my" spot in front of "my" tree!

Ecclesiastes 3: 4 says that there is a time to weep and a time to laugh, a time to mourn and a time to dance. I would look at the tree and tell myself that I would only allow myself to feel the way I did for a certain amount of time because I knew that God wanted a better life for me. I just didn't know how to do it. Everything seemed overwhelming. The days turned into weeks, and the weeks turned into months. However, as time passed, the tree started to look a little better. First it grew pretty pink flowers, and as summer came it filled so full of bright green leaves that you could barely see the branches that they grew on.

I realized that, like the tree, life changes. Nothing ever stays the same. Seasons come and go. People come and go. Heartaches come and go. I could look at things differently and focus on the good things in my life that God had given me.

By searching out the beauty around me, or in other people, my focus began to change. Instead of focusing on the things I couldn't change, I began trying to notice any positive I could, even if it was the smallest of things. Here are some examples:

- I have three healthy children who love me.
- I have a home of my own.
- I have a car that starts every day.
- I have a job.
- I have friends who care about me.
- I have a faith that carries me.

So even though everything changes, maybe we should just roll with those changes knowing that somehow things tend to work out and there is always something good to focus on instead. I took a picture of the tree when it was full of leaves as a reminder that changes will come. But in the end I pray that my life will be full because that's the way I choose to see it.

DAY 11

Touch Me

I have three children, and it amazes me how they are all so different in many ways. Once my oldest daughter was able to walk, she would stiffen up and aggressively wiggle her body out from my arms anytime I would try to snuggle with her or hold her. I would secretly wonder why she was like that. I think I needed to hold on to her more than she wanted to be held. She was perfectly happy though, so I let her be.

Then my second daughter was completely different. I pretty much carried her on my hip until she was four years old. I remember my then mother-in-law telling me that if I didn't put her down she would never walk. I cherished each day and the fact that she liked the comfort of my arms. I knew that eventually she would be grown and that I would miss those early days.

Then there is my son. He's a little bit of everything, but he has a kind heart and always makes me feel cared about. As they have gotten older, of course, any kind of hug in public is taboo. I don't mind because I remember being that way with my parents as well. It's a teenager "thing" I guess.

In *The Five Love Languages*, Gary Chapman explains that on some level we all have certain things about us that we want or need in order to feel loved or appreciated. If you break it down, most of us can be categorized into one or two of these languages. The thought is that we tend to treat others the way we want to be treated. If we observe how someone treats us, we see clues to what their love language is. For instance if your spouse or significant other is always giving you gifts, maybe that is a clue that they themselves love to get gifts.

Here are the languages:
- Acts of service
- Quality time
- Gifts
- Physical touch
- Words of affirmation

I think that over time our languages change depending on life experiences or just level of maturity. When I was young and in my first marriage, I admit now that I needed a lot of quality time because I had grown up in a home in which I felt invisible, and I needed attention to help me feel like I mattered. Now I feel almost smothered by the thought of having to spend so much time with someone. I have been so independent for so long now.

The thing I miss the most is touch. I am wired to want it. I do not recall any memory of my mom hugging me or saying that she loved me. Physical touch is something that I seem to need at the deepest level. There is something about someone hugging me that touches something deep within me. I'm not talking about a hug from a stranger because that can just be creepy! I mean a hug or a touch from someone who knows me and knows my heart. Maybe I like this person as a good friend, or maybe I might like them as more than a friend. Our hands can give so much when we use them to share how much we care about someone. Our hands can carry the power to end an argument or convey our love for someone in one moment if we use them in love.

A hug or a touch makes me feel cared about and protected. There are days when I feel like I am alone with nobody to protect me from whatever I am worried about. I am getting older, and I don't want to be alone the rest of my life. I long to give someone everything I have in this heart of mine, which as an adult who has experienced a lot includes:

- **Trust**. If we love someone, trust is the number one element that allows the other person to be himself or herself and allows them to live life to the fullest. And maybe, just maybe, it makes them love us more because we are saying to them, "I know you love me. Now go have fun because I know it is me that you will come home to."
- **My heart**. Once I love someone, nobody can divert my attention or make me want something different than what I have already been blessed with. Nobody is perfect, and I learned a long time ago that I am not going to make somebody change who they are.
- **Confidence**. I can spend a day by myself without worrying everything is going to fall apart if I don't spend each moment with the person I love.
- **Laughter**. Life is short, and things can change in a moment, so it is good to laugh whenever you can. It is essential.
- **Touch**. Without it, I keep the love that I was meant to give away to myself, and what good does that do?

So I remember the days when my children were young and I used my hands to nurture them or comfort them when they needed me. Now when my children surprise me with a hug out of the blue, or when someone I care deeply for touches me or wraps their arms around me in a protective way, my heart smiles. I am reminded how much I love them and how much I am loved in return.

Live Life
to the Fullest

D o you find yourself just doing the same things day in and day out never feeling any joy in your days? Why do we work so hard every day? We work hard to make money to pay our bills and of course to acquire more stuff. Some of us only have enough money to cover our bills and are barely getting by. We toil and we stress over every penny and how we will pay for this or that. We put off one bill to pay another that is more urgent, always with an undercurrent of dread that it will never get better.

We go to work each day and come home to take care of our families because we love them more than anything or anyone on this earth. But at the end of the day, we sometimes feel tired and weary.

John 10:10 says, "The thief comes only to steal and kill and destroy; I have come that they may have life and have it to the full."

Jesus came so that I could enjoy my life, so why am I not doing that? Who or what is the thief that is stealing my joy? It could be a myriad of things. Is it tiredness? Maybe I need more than six hours of sleep each night. Is it the people I'm hanging out with? Do they bring value to my life? Maybe it is my way of thinking that I am alone with no one to help me. At times I feel like I have the weight of the world on my shoulders.

But deep down I know better, so sometimes when I feel myself slipping, I pour myself a glass of red wine (or two) and reach way down into my soul to pull out the strength that resides inside of me. I have to remind myself not to worry about all of the "what ifs" and to live each day to the fullest. I have to remind myself that yes, I may feel lonely at night in my bed without someone's arm over me, but I have friends who care about me and children who love me.

I have to remember there are things in life that I have no control over, but I also need to take responsibility to be proactive in the things I can do. I don't want to be a slave to that thief that steals my joy any longer!

I want to seize each day and love those around me even in the littlest of ways. Once in a while I want to cherish a sunset or see a movie that makes me laugh with a friend who will laugh with me. Why can't I take a drive up to the mountains on the weekend for a day trip or to a winery for the day? Life shouldn't always be so filled with drudgery. I think I get stuck feeling that those things aren't as much fun without someone else. I guess I am an intimate creature by nature.

I have always dreamed of going to Tuscany with someone I love. Why do I sometimes feel like it will never happen? But if I go get my passport, am I not one step closer? I may not have the money to go now, but I am empowered by saving that little bit of money to get that passport, and maybe it will encourage me that such a trip is possible. I still park on one side of the garage and still sleep on one side of my bed because somehow I think if I park in the middle, or sleep in the middle, I am telling the universe there will never be room for someone else in my life again. So I keep my heart open even when it is tired and weary. I want to live this life that was given to me to the fullest—the way Jesus wanted it to be. I hope you do too.

If you feel like dancing, do it. I've been known to do this in my kitchen while I'm cooking.

If you feel like telling someone you love them, don't think about it; just do it.

If you feel like giving someone something, don't hesitate. It could be the Holy Spirit nudging you to do so.

If you feel like skinny-dipping in the lake, do it! (Don't get yourself arrested of course.)

If you feel like singing in the shower, belt it out like no one is around.

If you feel like crying, allow yourself. Sometimes it's just needed to wash out the pain and let in renewal.

Someday, I will lie in a bed of red poppies in Tuscany with someone I love, and I will have no shame in it. I will sing in the shower and dance in my kitchen and love those around me to the fullest. And I will have no regrets.

Do It Anyway

I wanted to share the following verses originally written by Kent Keith in his 1968 book *The Silent Revolution: Dynamic Leadership in the Student Council.* A version of them was painted on the wall of Mother Teresa's home for children in Calcutta, India, and other sources have repurposed and altered them over the years. They are so useful even in our own lives where we are surrounded by material wealth and luxury way more than others are around the world. Here is the version often attributed to Mother Teresa.

> People are often unreasonable, irrational, and self-centered. Forgive them anyway.
> If you are kind, people may accuse you of selfish, ulterior motives. Be kind anyway.
> If you are successful, you will win some unfaithful friends and some genuine enemies. Succeed anyway.
> If you are honest and sincere people may deceive you. Be honest and sincere anyway.
> What you spend years creating, others could destroy overnight. Create anyway.
> If you find serenity and happiness, some may be jealous. Be happy anyway.
> The good you do today will often be forgotten. Do good anyway.
> Give the best you have, and it will never be enough. Give your best anyway.

Aren't we created to live this way? Why do we spend our days so angry and disappointed with our lives when we could be doing good things with them? Be forgiving, love with everything we have inside of us. Give when we have the opportunity and even when we have little to give. Sometimes when we sacrifice, it actually means more.

When our friends are sick, bring them some soup. When they are discouraged, offer a big hug—not some puny one with a little tap-tap on the shoulder.

Life should be lived to the fullest, and you never know when it will be taken from us. So live it well, live it with love and joy and contentment for the people you have around you and every blessing that God has given, no matter how small and insignificant you may think those things are. Even when we don't feel like it, sometimes we just have to do it anyway!

Love Remains

"Now these three remain: faith, hope, and love.
But the greatest of these is love."
– Corinthians 13:14

I s it possible for someone to love us so much that when they die, they come back to us in a real way but in the form of their spirit? After they pass away, could they come to us in the form of a dream to comfort us? Is it possible that they come back as angels to watch over us until we meet them again?

I just finished reading a great book called *To Heaven and Back: A Doctor's Extraordinary Account of Her Death, Heaven, Angels, and Life Again* by Mary C. Neal, MD. I have always been fascinated by accounts from people after they have "near-death experiences." At times I was hesitant to believe fully; however, accounts I have read from small children are so similar that it's hard to disregard.

In Dr. Neal's book she stated, "The human brain is quite good at remembering events, but not usually so adept at remembering the precise details. If you ask most people to describe their wedding, a child's birth, or other such important life events, the tiny details will have faded and the stories will likely have changed some over time. Think about fishermen's tales, which grow with each telling, or the old-time game of "telephone" in which a story is whispered from one person to the next. The last person in line tells the story out loud and, when compared to the original version, is usually full of notable differences. Even vivid dreams rarely stay in our memories for more than a few minutes."

She went on to say, "I have observed one of the truly remarkable and consistent aspects of accounts of experiences that involve the presence or intervention of God is that the description of the experience remains constant no matter how much time has elapsed. People who have been involved in a Godly experience remember with clarity and constancy the details of the incident and vividly recall their emotions as though they had just occurred."

I was very close to my grandparents when I was young. When I was about twelve years old, I had a dream that I was lying on my grandparents' kitchen floor looking up at my grandmother's face as she looked down at me with tears streaming down her face. I awoke with the feeling that even though in my dream I was looking up, I felt like it was really my grandfather looking up. The thought of the dream stayed with me the next day as I was in school, and I wondered why I had such an intense dream. Toward the end of the day, my aunt pulled me out of class and took me back to her house, which was very out of the routine. I knew something wasn't right. I asked her if something had happened to my grandpa, and if so, why wasn't anyone telling me?

Of course, she assured me that everything was fine, but later I was told that my grandpa had died the night before of a heart attack on his kitchen floor. So many times over the years, I have thought about that dream. I wonder if he loved me so much that at the moment his soul left his body he came to me in my dream to let me know just how much he cared for me.

I still remember the dream so vividly after all these years later. I believe I remember it so well because it was a gift of love that is timeless. And like the verse in 1 Corinthians says, love remains!

Designed to Be Known

"O Lord, you have searched me and you know me. You know
when I sit and when I rise; you perceive my thoughts from afar.
You discern my going out and my lying down; you are familiar
with all my ways. Before a word is on my tongue you know it
completely, O Lord. You hem me in—behind and before; you have
laid your hand upon me. Such knowledge is too wonderful for me,
too lofty for me to attain. Where can I go from your Spirit? Where
can I flee from your presence? If I go up to the Heavens, you are
there; if I make my bed in the depths, you are there. If I rise on the
wings of the dawn, if I settle on the far side of the sea, even there
your hand will guide me; your right hand will hold me fast."
– Psalm 139: 1–10

The City of Loneliness—it's not a fun place to be. It can feel hopeless and desolate. It can feel like an echo, a crying out from your soul only to hear your own hurting voice crying back to you. Its streets have no laughter or joy. There is no sunshine, no gardens in bloom. The only sound we can hear is the sound of the wind that is so cold that it pierces us when we breathe in. We think that nobody knows our name in the City of Loneliness. We allow heartbreak to take our thoughts down dark alleyways where we lie awake at night thinking about everything that has gone wrong in our lives and how we aren't ever going to let anyone treat us this way or that way ever again. By doing this, we are closing the gates and locking ourselves in with heavy chains where nobody can get to us.

We feel like there is no way out and no hope of a better future because we keep looking over our shoulders at all the bad instead of looking ahead with even an ounce of positive thought. It's so easy to stay in this mode of travel—isn't it? But it doesn't have to be this way.

We hold the key to get out of this barren city. If the same God who created us knows us as the Psalm says, then why do we stay so negative in our minds? I can tell you why I presume this: because we choose not to read what He says to us in scripture, or if we do, we don't believe it whole-heartedly. We are flawed creatures, and we do not fully comprehend just how loved we are because we are so bound by the world around us. We were designed to be known. We were not designed to be living lives without the community of others, and when we shrink away into our loneliness, we close the door for others to love us because we think we are unworthy.

I think within all of us is a deep desire to be known, and whether we want to admit it or not, we like it when someone smiles at us or touches us. We like it when someone shows interest. Lord, let us out of this City of Loneliness and allow us to know just how deeply you love us.

Orphaned

I grew up in a home where I felt unwanted. I went through a marriage where I felt unwanted and unneeded. I am not saying this to paint a bad light on those who surrounded me. I say this to point out that I am the master of my thoughts and of the feelings that I ultimately carry for myself.

I am a grown woman who still to this day feels, well … orphaned. Don't feel sorry for me when I say this. I have good days, and I have my bad days. The good days outnumber the bad the majority of the time, but there are times when I can't get out of that negative feeling that I am alone and have no one to share my life with in the way that my heart has desired for my entire life. I call it "the funk." Even a new pair of shoes can't get me out of that funk!

I work hard each day, and I smile. But when my head hits my pillow at night, I'm lost. I count my blessings. I have a home and a job. My children are healthy and happy, but I find myself thinking that half of my life is over, and this is not how I pictured things to be. I want to be with someone who will say, "Come on! I'm taking us away for the weekend." I long for someone who makes me feel safe and protected, who can share the weight of the world with me. The darkness I feel on my pillow is a very empty feeling.

I think about when Jesus held the last supper with His friends and told them He would send them a helper and advocate when He was gone. That helper is the Holy Spirit. Jesus said, "If you love me, you will obey what I command. And I will ask the Father, and He will give you another Counselor to be with you forever—the Spirit of truth. The world cannot accept him. But you know him, for he lives with you and will be in you. I will not leave you as orphans; I will come to you" (John 14:15–18).

Think about this. Jesus knew His final day on this earth was approaching. He knew that He would suffer a painful death. These words must have been so important that He was telling His friends. Even though He was leaving this earth, He was telling them that as long as they obeyed His commandments and believed in Him, the Holy Spirit would come to them in times of need.

He went on to say in John 14:26–27, "But when the Counselor, the Holy Spirit, whom the Father will send in my name, will teach you all things and will remind you of everything I have said to you. Peace I leave with you; my peace I give you. I do not give to you as the world gives. Do not let your hearts be troubled and do not be afraid."

So when I feel alone and like an orphan, His words come to my mind and fill my heart. They remind me that He hasn't abandoned me at all. He lives inside of me, and no matter where life takes me or no matter how dark things feel, He is a constant light to guide me. I just need to trust that His plans for me are greater than I can even imagine, and I am not an orphan at all.

DAY 17

A Life without Faith

*"He called a little child and had him stand among them.
And then he said: 'I tell you the truth, unless you change
and become like little children, you will never enter the
Kingdom of Heaven. Therefore, whoever humbles himself
like this child is the greatest in the Kingdom of Heaven.'"*
– Matthew 18:2–4

I know that we all have different degrees of faith or different levels of beliefs. I know that there are some who do not believe in God at all, and it is not for me to judge those people. I can only try to live right and maybe be a light to someone else. I am definitely not a perfect person by any means, and I have made my fair share of mistakes. Perhaps I am here only to plant a little seed in someone's heart to get them thinking about God and the possibility that maybe, just maybe He does exist.

Not long ago I had a discussion with someone whom I have known a very long time, and I asked them, "Don't you believe that Jesus was the Son of God?" They very matter-of-factly said that they did not and that they believed people made up religion to make themselves comfortable. They stated that religion was for the "simple minded." This sounded to me like they were saying that to believe in such a thing made me stupid. I pondered the statement for a while and then offered the question, "Even if you were on your death bed and given the opportunity to accept Christ, you would not do it?" The answer was, "No, I do not think so."

I had a mixture of emotions that I felt compelled to hide, but inside I was torn up. I wanted to scream and shake sense into this person. Then in the next moment I wanted to cry and plead with them, "Do you know what you just said?" I felt troubled for them and for the fact that I didn't know what to say to change their mind. I felt like maybe I let God down because I didn't know how to defend Him.

Mark Batterson, author of *Wild Goose Chase*, a book about reclaiming the pursuit of God, writes about how we have forgotten to realize how the Holy Spirit still works in our lives today. He wrote: "Faith is not logical. But it isn't illogical either. Faith is theological. It does not ignore reality; it just adds God into the equation." He goes on to say: "Faith is not mindless ignorance; it simply refuses to limit God to the logical constraints of the left brain. Think of it this way. Logic questions God. Faith questions assumptions. And at the end of the day, faith is to trust God more than you trust your own assumptions."

It is easy to be discouraged. It is easy to put God in a box and say we can figure things out on our own. It is easy to think we are in control, but the longer I live, I realize I'm not in control of very much at all. Life is an adventure or a disappointment. It's depressing or can bring us great moments of joy, which are usually found in the little things.

Life, like faith, can be viewed how we choose to see it. I choose to believe like a little child that He does exist and is in control, even if I don't understand where He is bringing me. Relinquishing my control allows me to see things, situations, and people in a different light. I pray my friend will find that peace and will eventually believe as well.

In Case of an Emergency

I put a bucket list together recently, and the first thing listed was to get my passport. I am happy to report that it took a while, but it finally arrived. YES! I was a happy girl even though I have no way of getting to Italy right now. However, I am one step closer than I was.

There was a section on the application where I needed to fill out who I would want to call in case of an emergency. When married, I would have put my husband down without hesitation. I sat there and looked at the blank page and thought, "Who would come for me if I needed them?" It was a sobering question.

Who would come for you? I remember my grandmother telling me when I was young that over my life I would make many acquaintances but very few friends. She was so right. I can count on one hand my truest friends. I know they would drop everything to help me, and I would do the same for them. I love them. I value them. I am thankful for them more than they probably know.

This brings me to another question. Whom do you spend your time with? I've heard the saying that we are only as good as those we surround ourselves with. Do we bring value to their lives, and do they bring value to ours? Are the people we hang out with shallow? Are they interested in what really matters in life? Do they inspire us, or do they just fill up time in our days? I can go out dancing and be happy, but I know there is so much more to life than doing that every single weekend. I need quiet time to be alone as well as having a real conversation with someone face to face about anything and everything. At times, I need time to connect to God or nature.

I believe we all want to be known by someone—not the exteriors we put on, but the real us, the gritty, funny, sad, angry, or whatever-may-be us. I realize that someday our exterior appearances will change no matter how much time we spend on the treadmill or at the gym. Our bodies change. Our faces change. Our hair becomes gray. (I will fight this as long as possible!) I want to know that even when those things happen, I will have friends who love me no matter what. We may see them with our eyes, but better yet we will be able to see their hearts and the people they are on the inside. What greater joy could we find than that?

So who's your in-case-of-emergency person? If you don't know, be a friend who cares and see how the universe will bring someone to you who cares about you as well.

The Empty Nest

*"Train a child in the way he should go,
and when he is old he will not turn from it."*
– Proverbs 22:6

It seems like just yesterday when my children were small. It seems like just yesterday that I felt like I did not have a moment to myself to even finish a whole thought in my head before someone was calling out my name, "Mom!"

I remember the sleepless nights and the thousands of diapers I must have changed. I recall the temper-tantrums and taking my baby in the bathroom in her bouncy chair just so I could take a shower. A trip to the grocery store alone was like a vacation!

I remember people telling me to embrace those days because they would be gone before I knew it. Here I am, twenty-three years later. Despite all of those times when I felt overwhelmed or under-qualified to be a mother, I feel so blessed that I was able to spend all those years at home raising them. I would not have wanted anyone else on this earth to do it for me.

The funny thing is, when I look back over those years, it really isn't the negative things I reflect on. I think about the sound of their laughter and how they would find delight in the littlest of things. I think about the times when I would rock them to sleep in my blue rocker in a moonlit room and the smell of their fresh bathed skin. They would fall asleep but instead of putting them in the crib, I would hold on to them just a little bit longer as they dreamed.

I think about how I would press my lips to their temples to see if they had a fever. I still do that today, but they don't like it. Teenagers are like that I guess. Now we aren't allowed to touch them at all!

I think about how I would know how one of them was feeling without a word even being spoken. Parents just have intuition about some things. I remember the countless nights I laid down with them at bedtime to read the same book over and over again. I often contemplated secretly that we might have to "lose" the book one night.

My friends were right. Time did go by fast. Mistakes were made I'm sure, but I still loved them. I knew it was my job to raise my children in a way to give them their wings, so that when it was time to leave my nest, they would be able to soar. I want my children to have a good life and not to feel guilty when they leave me. I want them to know that I will always love them and will always be here for them.

They are not all gone yet, but I can feel it coming, and my heart aches for that loss of what I have known for the last twenty-three years, but with that I pray that I have equipped them with what is most important: to live good lives of integrity, honor, and faith. The world puts so much emphasis on material wealth and pleasure. There is nothing wrong with either one, but all things must be balanced. I hope that when they do leave this nest, they will carry me with them in their hearts. I hope they will remember what I have told them, for they are truly the loves of my life, and I wouldn't trade a single moment.

More

Watch out! Be on your guard against all kinds of greed; a man's life does not consist in the abundance of his possessions."
– Luke 12:15

One day I saw a bumper sticker that said, "The One with The Most Toys Wins!" Why do we spend so much time collecting stuff and acquiring so many things? Do those things really make us happy? Perhaps they do momentarily until we find the next best thing to strive for. We end up having to work hard to pay for all of our things and in turn become slaves to our debt. We then wonder if it was really worth it.

I've never really been a "things" girl, and as I have gotten older, I find myself giving away more and more. I work hard to pay my bills, and I live a very simple life. I do not have everything I want, but I do have everything I need. For that I am grateful.

There are some hard choices I must make in the very near future. It is overwhelming to not have someone to guide me. I may not be able to keep my house that I worked so hard for—the house that I vowed to my children would be our home. I've spent countless hours painting, gardening, and sewing window treatments to make it cozy. I've spent many fall evenings on my patio with good friends who have become so close to me.

My pride is holding on tight, but my heart is telling me that in order to have less stress I might have to sell it and find something smaller. My heart is telling me that maybe God wants something MORE for me, but if my hands are gripping so tight to this, they will not be open for what He may have in store for me.

God reminded me the other night that everything I have really is a gift from Him anyway. So I have started letting go of my grip little by little. I have cleaned out my closets and given lots away to the Salvation Army. I've thrown away so many things I know I will never use again. In the process I have begun to open to the idea that He has never left me before and that He will watch over me and guide my steps when I feel confused.

The more I give away, the more I realize that I really do not need those things to fill up my life. What I really need more of is HIM!

Why Cry?

Why do we cry? Is it any less manly for a guy to cry? Why would it be? Were we not created to feel emotion on many levels? It is one thing that differentiates us from other species. Crying has been proven to relieve stress and reduce certain hormones and chemical levels in the body, which helps return us to a calm state.

Some people see crying as a sign of weakness, but in certain situations, I feel it is anything but that. Look at what Ecclesiastes 3:1–8 says:

> There is a time for everything,
> and a season for every activity under heaven.
> a time to be born and a time to die,
> a time to plant and time to uproot,
> a time to kill and a time to heal,
> a time to tear down and a time to build,
> a time to weep and a time to laugh,
> a time to mourn and a time to dance,
> a time to scatter stones and a time to gather them,
> a time to embrace and a time to refrain,
> a time to search and a time to give up,
> a time to keep and a time to throw away,
> a time to tear and time to mend,
> a time to be silent and a time to speak,
> a time to love and a time to hate,
> a time to war and a time for peace.

It also goes on to say that God has set eternity in the hearts of men. Maybe this is why we sometimes feel that raw loneliness, a longing to be known and loved. We each have this hole in our heart that is longing for eternity and the love that it would encompass. We all long to be loved by someone else whether we want to admit it or not. I believe it is hard wired in each of us. The scripture says it is set in our hearts.

Life can be taken from us in an instant, so laugh when you are happy. Cry happy tears, or cry sad tears. They are liberating and cleanse our souls! Dance like no one is watching and tell someone you love them even if you don't think it will be said back to you. It is good to be authentic, and there can be no regrets in doing that.

It's More Than Just Dinner

"Supper is about prevention and repair. We don't have to reinvent our relationships every day because they are already built into what we know we will do. We don't have to make a special time to get together because it already exists. We have a place where we can bring things, a set of actions that is both symbolic and real."
– Miriam Weinstein

There were two types of dinners I experienced as a child. They were stark in contrast, yet both left a lasting impression on me. One type of dinner I had was with my mother and stepfather. It was laden with rules, over-sized portions, and tension so thick even our steak knives could not cut through it. There was no talk about how your day was because quite frankly children in our house were to be seen and never heard. It was silent except for the few derogatory comments my forever-unhappy stepfather would say. It was a time to eat as fast as you could, so you could disappear back into your room, away from the threat of ugly words and probably some sort of punishment from out of nowhere.

Then there was dinner at my best friend's house. They ate every evening at 6:00 p.m. It was a set time, and there were no questions where they would be at that time of day. No matter what adventure she and I were into, she always had to go home by six. I ate a lot of dinners at her house growing up, and I loved every one of them. At first I thought it was odd they ate every day together because our house was so sporadic and without routine of any sort. I also found it interesting they talked to each other while they ate. But over time I concluded that one day when I had a family, dinnertime would be important. It would be a time to let my children know they are loved and cared for. It would be a place to come together and feel like a family should feel.

It's funny the things we remember as children and the decisions we make based on our experiences. We can have self-pity and carry on the bad habits and negative traits, or we can choose to make different paths. We can create better experiences for the ones we love and for ourselves. We have the power to break the domino effect that others carried on before us and to live a better life.

So I choose to say thank you, Laurel, for being my friend since we were eight or nine years old and sharing your family with me. It changed me and showed me a different life. It showed me the importance of family tradition, love, and character. It showed me the power of our minds, and if we change the way we think, our actions will follow suit.

I hope my children will look back some day and feel thankful for all of the meals we shared over their lifetime. I hope they realize why I made it such an important part of our lives.

I Come as I Am

I wasn't going to go to church this morning. I reasoned with myself that I hadn't gone consistently in the last few months. I didn't want to go by myself and be reminded of how alone I was. I thought about how much I loved going to church with my husband and how good it felt when we were there together. I thought about how good it felt when he would squeeze my hand and put his arm around me as we worshiped.

I also reasoned with myself that if I continued on this path of becoming comfortable with withdrawing from others, I would eventually become an island where no one could get to me at all. Admittedly, that sounds kind of good at times, but not good for my spirit I am sure.

So reluctantly I got up and got ready, all the while asking God to help me see Him in my life because He seemed so distant at times. I know deep within that He is not distant, but lately I just do not feel it.

As I walked into service, I observed everyone who was around me, keenly aware of my singleness. I know it doesn't make me insignificant; I was just acutely aware. Then the worship began, and the words in the song "I come as I am" sunk so deeply. Yes, I came even though I didn't want to. I came alone and afraid of my future. I came full of worry, but I came and I decided it was a step in the right direction.

The energy is always good at my church. The pastor always seems genuine, and his heart seems in the right place.

The sermon was about how to be grateful:

1. Alertness—our eyes have to be open each day to the miracles around us, to the Holy Spirit working around us and in us. If we walk around complaining and only seeing the negative, then we are not alert to what He may be trying to show us every day.

2. Attire—what clothes do we put on spiritually every day? Anxiety? Bitterness? Loneliness? (Yes, yes, and yes, I was ashamed to admit this to myself.)

3. Access—Isaiah 52:2 says to rise from the dust and remove the chains of slavery. Shake off the dust when someone hurts you or criticizes you. Don't allow negative thoughts to access your heart. Be armed for the battle!

So I am grateful today that I shook off the dust and drove myself to church. It was a timely reminder that I needed to change my way of thinking and get back to the strong person I know I am. It reminded me that He is still with me even though I do not have a physical human being to squeeze my hand or put their arm around me each day.

I have the King of Kings within me, and I come to Him as I am. He accepts that with more love than any human can. I come to Him just as I am, and He accepts that.

DAY 24

Dreams

"Dreams are important. They're messages from God.
When you ignore them or resist them or are kept from
pursuing them, you are cut to the core of your being."
– Glenn Beck

I have often thought we have dreams and desires in our hearts for a reason. They are what we constantly think about or wish we could do or be.

If our dreams are messages from God, then maybe we need to believe that if we take even the smallest of steps to make those dreams and desires happen, He will guide us each step of the way.

The longer I live, I have come to believe there are no coincidences. Perhaps He guides us when we observe what is happening around us. Perhaps He brings other people into view and into our lives in order for us to learn something.

With our eyes open, we must keep dreaming and being aware. He might just be guiding you the whole way.

Disappointment

There will be times in our lives that we will be disappointed. That's a guarantee, but it will be our choice if we let those things make us live in the hopeless feeling of discouragement. When we are tired, hungry, or discouraged is when we tend to make poor choices. Trust me—I've made mistakes at those exact times.

So renew your mind when disappointment comes and know that you are never alone. If we are believers in the one true God, we must also believe He lives within us and we are never alone.

Cracked and Beautiful

I would like to share an old folktale that illustrates God's view of our brokenness. It is called "The Water Bearer."

A water bearer in India had two large pots: each pot hung on one end of a pole that the man carried across his neck. One of the pots had a crack in it, while the other pot was perfect. The perfect pot always arrived full at the end of the long walk from the stream to the master's house, while the cracked pot arrived only half full.

This daily trek continued for two full years. Of course, the perfect pot was proud of its accomplishments, fulfilling the task it was created for. But the poor cracked pot was ashamed of its flaws, miserable that it fell short of perfection. One day the flawed pot spoke to the water bearer of its sadness. "I am ashamed of myself, and I want to apologize to you." "Why?" asked the bearer.

"I have only been able, for the past two years, to carry half my load because the crack in my side causes water to leak out all the way back to your master's house. Because of my flaws, you have to do all this work, and you don't get the full value for your efforts," the pot said.

The water bearer felt sorry for the old cracked pot. And in his compassion he said, "As we return to the master's house I want you to notice the beautiful flowers along the path."

Indeed, as they went up the hill, the old cracked pot took notice of the sun warming the beautiful wildflowers on the side of the path, and this cheered it some. But at the end of the trail, it still felt the pang of sadness because it had leaked out half its load, and so again it apologized to the bearer for its failure.

Then the bearer asked, "Did you notice that there were flowers only on your side of the path, but none on the other pot's side?" The pot nodded.

"That's because I have always known about your flaw, and I took advantage of it. I planted flower seeds on your side of the path, and every day while we walked back from the stream, you've watered them. For two years I have been able to pick these beautiful flowers to decorate my master's table. If you were not created this way, my master would not have had this beauty grace his house."

Aren't we a bunch of *cracked pots*? I didn't say crackpots; I said cracked pots! Each of us has our own unique flaws. Sometimes we walk around with a self-defeating frame of mind. We tell ourselves that we are worthless because of our pasts. Life sometimes seems meaningless because it hasn't turned out the way we dreamt it would.

I love this story about the cracked pot because it makes me think of God as the water bearer. He knows our flaws and loves us anyway. He can take our flaws and make something beautiful out of them. He knows the potential in us. How can we help others when they are hurting if we have not experienced hurt ourselves? Our hurts, pains, and struggles can make us stronger and able to help others who might be going through something similar.

"Yet, O Lord, you are our Father. We are the clay, you are the potter; we are all the work of your hand" (Isaiah 64:8).

Peace

"Peace: it does not mean to be in a place where there is no noise, trouble, or hard work. It means to be in the midst of those things and still be calm in your heart."
– Author Unknown

There is a painting done by Jack E. Dawson called "Peace in the Midst of the Storm." You can find it on his website jackdawson.com. In his painting, a small bird sits peacefully under the rushing waterfalls. There are other things hidden in the picture if we look carefully. But my main focus is how calm the bird is even though everything around it seems loud and chaotic.

I want to feel peace when storms come. There have been times when I let the storms shake and fill me with fear, not knowing which way to turn. They made me feel like giving up. But after going through those times, I realize that I made some wrong decisions when I let fear be my guide. When I allowed fear to guide my choices, I was disconnected from my source. I was not trusting God. Going forward, I learned to recognize if I was doing or not doing something out of fear or if I had a peace about what was happening. Let peace be your guide and you can weather any storm.

A Different Outlook

As I look out my window into the back yard each day, I see my two plum trees bare from the winter. Gray and without leaves, they fit in with the rest of the landscape that lies in hibernation. To say the least, it has been a rough year, and when I see those trees I think to myself that spring is coming, and with it, new life will begin to bloom. I wonder to myself if my life will ever do the same.

I had been allowing fear and worry to take hold of me. My marriage was officially over, my fence was falling apart, my truck kept breaking, the garage door worked only when it wanted to, my refrigerator broke, and so forth. Every time I thought I could get ahead, something kicked me five steps back. I fell behind in my mortgage and couldn't recover. I didn't ask for help. I felt truly defeated for the first time in a very long time.

This woman who loved to garden, write, and paint let her yard get out of hand and stopped writing her manuscript. She put her easel away, and hope seemed extinguished.

It took some hard lessons, but I turned around my thinking and got a second job. I had good friends who encouraged me. I will never forget my friend who said, "Dori, you are letting everything overwhelm you. Just take one room at a time. If something is broken in that room, work on fixing that and nothing else. With that accomplished, you will feel better. Then move on to the next room. You can do this!" Another friend had someone come fix my fridge, and another friend sent someone to fix my garage door.

The burdens were lifting, and so were my spirits. The flame in my spirit seemed to be reignited. I decided to apply for a loan modification to see if I could get my mortgage back in order. The mortgage company approved the modification, and my mortgage became current after many months of not being able to make my payments.

I will not always be this alone, and things will not look so grim. I choose to be grateful each morning even before my feet hit the floor. I say thank you to the Lord that I have this bed to keep me warm at night. I say thank you to the Lord for my children and our health. I say thank you to the Lord for bringing friends into my life who shine light onto me. I say thank you to the Lord for my abundance because I believe that is what I have.

So as the New Year began, I had a new outlook on my situation. I planted new flowers in the spring, worked on my manuscript, and painted with a glass of wine in hand. I knew that I was not alone.

DAY 29

Draw Close

I withdraw from the noise and the crowd
To hear your voice
Where it is not so loud
I withdraw from the endless chatter
The surface-level talk
To hear and read the words that matter
I withdraw from what the world searches for and will never find
To you Lord
With your arms outstretched and your heart so kind
– Dori Grassau

Being single has its ups and downs. I admit that I like having my closet all to myself. I like being able to rearrange my furniture any way I like it. I like having complete control of the remote! I like being able to come and go as I please. I am not a stranger to being alone because I spent almost my entire childhood perfecting it due to my family dynamics. I am confident in who I am without anyone. I know that I am a child of God first and foremost. Therefore, I know that ultimately I am not truly alone.

However, I realize that sometimes I can get swept away with being busy all of the time. Between working full time and having children to take care of, there seems to be little time to really be still and reflect about where my life is going and if I am making a difference. Am I doing what I know in my heart I have been called to do, or am I filling my days with noise and business? Am I spending time with people who are chasing the wrong things and are surface-level only?

I feel a sense of urgency lately to do those things I am wired to do—those things that bring me joy when I do them. Write, cook, paint, or spend time at the beach. Over the last several months, I have been making time to be still and hear God's small voice within me. I believe we all have the capability to hear it if we withdraw to draw close. If we withdraw for a time to search out our purpose without the noise and distractions, I believe that God always gives us answers. Sometimes it's in a song we hear or a person who speaks to us about matters of the heart. Sometimes just being in nature's beauty we can "hear" Him. James 4:8 says, "Come near to God and He will come near to you."

So for now I withdraw to draw close. I write, paint, and cook. I spend time with the people whom I love and who love me back. I rearrange my priorities and begin to look at how I can help others now instead of seeking out the help of others. I draw close, so He can bring His best to me because I am no longer seeking the wrong things or the wrong people.

I can accept that if it is meant to be, I will not always be single. No matter how good I am at being single, I love seeing a man's clothes in the closet next to mine and hearing the sound of football on my television. I sometimes need a man's strong arms to move that furniture and put his arms around me from behind when I am cooking.

So today I withdraw to draw close.

DAY 30

Honor Your Father and Mother

How do we do this when they have abandoned us? Maybe physically or emotionally they have not been there. We have just been written off as unwanted. Perhaps there is more to the story than we know. Maybe somewhere along the way they were small and innocent as everyone once is, and someone hurt them. Perhaps they did not have the tools they needed in order to heal. Perhaps it was their own choice not to heal because it allowed them to feel justified in their misery. There will always be unanswered questions.

Ephesians 6:1–3 says, "Children, obey your parents in the Lord, for this is right. Honor your father and mother is the first commandment with a promise—that it may go well with you and that you may enjoy long life on the earth."

What a tough pill to swallow at times. Why should I honor someone who hurt me so much? In a loving family, I surmise this is easy. In a loving family, our parents provide protection, discipline, guidance, and teaching. They give us those things because they love us. When we take heed to their guidance, it indeed keeps us safer, longer, in exact accordance to this scripture verse.

I will tell you why we must swallow this pill regardless of how we have been treated or not treated.

I have known parents who have loved their children and have done their best to guide them the best they know how, yet the children still choose to go their own ways even if it is to their own detriment. They forget about their parents as they age and choose not to take care of them when they need protection. These are the same parents who provided for and protected them when they were young, yet it does not matter. This is nothing less than sad to me.

Being a parent has opened my eyes to the fact that we are human. I've made mistakes, I have hurt, and I have questioned if I am doing a good enough job with my children. I too feel like maybe I did not have the tools to do the "perfect" job, but in the same sense, I know that God gave those children to me and I was chosen for them. It is my duty to do the best that I know how, and somehow it has to be enough.

My mom hurt me; I admit this. I do not want to dishonor her by slandering her in any way. I could sit here and create a list of all the things she said or did that hurt me, but what good would it do?

Recently I decided to refinish two very old windows that were in pretty bad shape but had good potential. I took the time to clean them up. Old glue was scraped off of the glass panes and holes were filled with wood putty. Fresh paint was applied. I dipped some old dresser knobs into crushed sea glass and added them as décor. Pictures were carefully chosen to put behind each pane.

I do not have much family, so I wanted pictures that had significance. I came across the sweetest picture of my mother at age three. It was in sepia and she had the sweetest expression on her face as she sat with her hands in her lap posed for the picture. Her dark hair was long with a section of it braided up around the crown of her head. How could I remain angry with her when looking at this?

I know that once she was a little girl, and something went horribly wrong. Thinking of her as a child somehow lessens the pain for me. It creates empathy and grace. It allows me to honor her, even if it is from afar. In honoring her, it allows me to love her, which in the end heals me.

Doing Love

I woke up yesterday with a good healthy anger. It's the kind of anger that motivates you to change. It's where you say, "Lord, change my situation or change me! Show me which way to go. I can't do this without You anymore!"

I am no longer going to sit around and wait for love to find me. Do I want someone to love and care for? Yes. Do I want someone to love and care for me? Yes. There are other things that have not fallen into place for me either, but my outlook has turned the proverbial corner. I do not want to just let life throw me about like waves on the ocean this way and that. The storm has carried on too long. I want to do and be love—toward my children, my coworkers, my friends, and strangers. If that makes me seem crazy, then strap on the straight jacket!

If that means being alone, then so be it. If someone can't hug me and put their arms around me before I go to sleep at night, then I will hug someone else who needs it. If someone won't kiss me when I need it most, then I will kiss my dog on the forehead just because I can!

A health scare will put us in a reflective mode more than anything else. Financial distress or a loss will do the same. It makes you have this sense of urgency to make your life somehow worthwhile. You begin to live life on purpose. You realize and accept there are things you can change and things you can't. You begin to choose more carefully what you say and what you do.

I have never been a big party girl, even though there was a brief period of time I stepped out on the edge of that. But each time I would be driving home from those events a little part of me would think, why did I do this tonight? I never overindulged in anything and was usually the first one to leave when everyone else stayed until the wee hours in the morning. I doubted if I really fit in. It didn't feel like love. It felt empty and shallow. This might not be someone else's view, but it was my individual experience. I love to go out and be around others. It just depends on the environment sometimes.

Doubt comes in many forms and during many trials. James 1:2–3 says, "Consider it pure joy, my brothers, whenever you face trials of many kinds, because you know that the testing of your faith develops perseverance."

It doesn't say *if* we face trials; it says *when*. It goes on in verse 6 to say that we must believe and not doubt because those who doubt are like a wave of the sea, blown and tossed by the wind.

I will persevere by being busy doing and being love. For when we are distracted by the right things, we are filled with joy. And along the way, I think *love finds us* whether through other people or the satisfaction that we did what we are here on this earth to do.

So my friends, stop *looking* for love and start *doing* love!

DAY 32

Caged Bird

When I was a little girl we had parakeets. I remember how each of them had very different and distinct personalities. Freda was more aggressive and wouldn't let me hold her. She would peck at the other birds and at me if I came near. It would humor me just to put my finger in the cage because the closer my finger got to her, the farther back she would lean, almost to the point where she would be hanging upside down still grasping tightly to the perch with her little feet.

Bubbles, on the other hand, always wanted to sit on my finger or my shoulder. He would let me take him with me all around the house. My brother was six years younger than I was, and I recall him putting Bubbles in the front cab of his metal Tonka truck and "driving" him all around the floors in the house. All the while, Freda was perfectly happy being left alone in the cage.

On occasion, my mom would trim their wings down and leave the cage open for them to be able to step out on the perches and landings she had created on the outside of the cage. I would ask her, "Mom, why are you cutting their wings?" Of course she would explain that it was so that they wouldn't be able to fly all over the house. But part of me felt that they should be able to fly. After all, that is what they were made to do. They weren't created to sit in that cage. They weren't created to not spread their wings and soar.

The reflective part of me thinks now about Freda. Maybe she became bitter that she had been put in that cage. She was so angry that even when given the opportunity for freedom, she couldn't take it because she didn't know anything else. Her mind was closed to the potential of getting out. Day after day, she sat on her perch watching the other birds stepping out.

I can still see Bubbles's light blue and white feathers all fluffed up while the wind flew through them as my brother drove him around. Perhaps he knew that it was the only way he could feel those winds since he could not fly himself.

So many days I have felt like that caged bird in my marriage, in my work, in my daily life. We get up and do the same things day in and day out, but inside we know we were created for more. People come along and want to take us out of the cage, and we peck at them because we have become bitter or are afraid to love and be hurt again. Lord, how I want to fly. Lord, how I want to live my life the way I was created to live.

I'm tired of these clipped wings and being a caged bird. Let me spread my wings and soar to the places you want me to go. I am created for so much more.

Burn Baby Burn

From a few childhood experiences and well into my adult life, I have found that each trial or disappointment I have gone through has in some way refined me like fire refines silver. Have the trials been fun? They definitely have not been fun. Have they changed the way I react to situations and to people? Yes.

There have been mistakes and hardships along the way that have hurt me, as well as others. There has been anger and sadness, and oh how it burned when things did not go "as planned."

One of the items on my bucket list is to have a shiny silver convertible. I like the idea of silver over any other color. Zechariah 13:9 says, "This third I will bring into the fire; I will refine them like silver and test them like gold. They will call on my name, and I will answer them. I will say, 'They are my people,' and they will say, 'The Lord is our God.'"

It is when we go through tough times that we are refined by them. Perhaps each burning makes us a little more pure. But the most important thing I notice is that God doesn't abandon us. He takes us through it, so we can get to the other side. Sometimes the way seems so unclear and foggy, but at least He is with us. It gives me hope to keep on enduring.

I have found that when we are going through that fire or trial is when most people finally call out to God for help. It may not be in our timing or in our ways, but help does come.

So with each burning, we become a little more refined. We become more patient, kinder, better listeners, and less judging of others. We realize how short life really is and are more aware of what we do with our time and our lives. We begin to live on purpose and with passion.

Someday I am going to have that silver convertible. I do not know when or how, but I can see it now, just on the other side of this burning fire called my life.

Wanted versus Needed

Y ou would think that I—a woman who loves to nurture others—would thrive on being needed, but I don't. I do want to be wanted though. If I truly believe that God is all I need, then anyone else is a bonus.

I feel that being chosen and wanted is so much better then being needed. Being wanted or wanting someone is a more mature, less codependent view of someone. Viewing them this way makes them your partner, confidant, playmate, and soulmate.

The constraints of a "relationship" are loosened, and we are free to grow and be who we are with each other. We trust the other person and feel security, and in turn, it is given back to us.

I say all this because growing up I felt very unwanted. My mother may have loved me, but I never felt it. She had the option of aborting me but chose not to. For that I am thankful and believe that because of that my life has some sort of relevance.

I needed her more than words can say at times. I still miss her and the affection that was never given but always wanted.

You see I needed her, but I felt like she never wanted me. They are two different things.

As an adult, I want to love someone for whom they are. I'm not in the business of changing anyone. People can only change themselves.

I want to see the good in others because essentially I think we all have good inside of us.

I want to cook for someone because it brings me joy.

I want fresh flowers on the table because they make me smile and remind me of God's creations.

I want someone's touch because it makes me feel alive!

I admit there are many things I need, but I realize all of my needs get taken care of eventually.

My wants are just icing on the cake when they come.

Breathe In
& Breathe Out

Sometimes I realize how anxious my heart can be. I worry about my children as they get older in different ways than I did when they were little. When they were little, I could control their world in most ways. I felt like I could protect them from anything.

But now as they begin to leave the nest, I find myself stopping. I pause to breathe in and breathe out when I feel that pang of realization that they will soon be gone. Even with the stresses of raising them mostly on my own and the financial strain, I wouldn't have traded it for anything.

It's a different feeling when your son or daughter begins to drive and has freedom like never before. It's a different feeling when someone breaks their hearts and there's nothing you can do about it. Sometimes they just want you to listen when all you want to do is go hunt the person down! Therefore, I just breathe in and I breathe out.

As a parent, you hope that you did things more right than wrong and that they will realize everything you did was out of love. You hope they will one day have mercy on you for the mistakes you did make along the way. You hope they will gain understanding about all the times you said no to them and made them so mad. They do not realize how many times I remained silent. I breathed in and I breathed out, choosing my battles wisely.

I hope that when I asked for forgiveness, they not only saw a mom but also a person who was trying their best. I hope they see someone who was willing to admit when they were wrong. I tried to raise them the best way I knew how, having little guidance myself growing up.

So with each passing day and with each worry, I will keep reminding myself that I am not alone. I know I have a God who watches over and guides me. As they get closer and closer to a life on their own, I will release them to be the beautiful souls they are. And when I feel that pang, I will breathe in and I will breathe out.

Today I Saw

How many of us go through our days without really noticing what is going on around us? We wake up and get ready to go to jobs we are less-than-passionate about. We sit in traffic, we work, and then we get back in traffic. We take care of our duties at home, and if we are lucky we find something or someone to enjoy before the day is over.

Today I wanted to really be present in each moment.

Today I saw a couple in the coffee shop looking at each other as they took sips of their coffee. A song came on, and they both wiggled their heads to the beat while still gazing at each other with big huge grins on their faces. It made me smile too. It also made me feel a little jealous.

I saw a redbird perched on my feeder as I looked out my back door as I do every morning. I always think he is there just for me.

I saw women whispering about others in an unkind way. It saddened me.

I saw my friend's eyes well up when she realized she almost ran me over with her car. I felt mercy.

I breathed in the smell of the rain as it poured down on my umbrella. I felt thankful.

I saw my son's face light up when he got a new pair of basketball shoes. I felt impressed that it took so little to make him happy.

I saw an elderly couple in the doctor's office smiling at each other and walking arm-in-arm as they left. I wanted to know their story.

Lord, I just want to be present in this very moment. Please don't let me be blind to life just passing me by. Please let me love everyone to the best of my ability as a mother, a friend, a coworker, and a sister.

There are so many things I have worked for and strived for. I know I will get there eventually, but I don't want to miss the scenery along the way. Today I saw that God has a plan for me, and whatever it is, I accept it.

When You're Ready for Me

When you're ready for me
Come take my hand, and we will carry life's
burdens together.

I will take your flaws if you agree to take mine too.
Do not try to change me, and I will not try to change you.

Lovingly challenge me to pursue my dreams, and I will
challenge you to do the same.

Kiss me and hug me every day, for it makes me feel alive and
forget the pain.

Pursue me even when you know that you've had me all along.
Hold me tight now and don't let me go, for when you are
finally ready, I might already be gone.

Thankful

I love Thanksgiving more than any other holiday. It's not about what someone is going to buy us. It's all about taking note of what or whom we are grateful for in our lives. It's a time to take stock of what really matters. It's so easy to get caught up in thinking about all that has gone wrong or all the things we wish we could have or achieve.

I have been trying very hard to change that way of thinking. Every time I have a negative thought pop into my head, I try to replace it with something positive. This takes practice. I work in a doctor's office, and every day I see someone who is sick or ailing. I think to myself how blessed I am to be healthy. I am not saying this to brag but to humble myself because I know things can change in an instant and want to appreciate the health I have. I walk past people in wheel chairs or people who can barely walk, and I am again thankful that I still have the use of my legs and hands. I realize there are so many things I take for granted.

What do you think you would notice if you put your phone down, shut off your television, or went for a walk? What would remind you of something that you are thankful for?

I am thankful for the smell of the fresh crisp air on a fall day.

I am thankful for the sound of my children laughing. There is no better sound.

I am thankful I have a roof over my head when there are many who do not.

I am thankful that my coworkers smile at me each day. It makes my day more tolerable.

I am thankful for each sunset that I see in this North Carolina sky. I have always said that God is the best artist. No one can paint a picture better that what He has created.

I am thankful that I have friends who care for me.

Those are just a few things, but I challenge you to make a list of the things you are thankful for and tape it to your bathroom mirror where you can see it at the beginning of each day. You will be amazed at how life doesn't seem so bad if you remind yourself each day of all the blessings you already have.

"Give thanks to the Lord, for he is good; his love endures forever" (1 Chronicles 16:34).

DAY 39

The Bucket List
Living Life Intentionally

"The question isn't who is going to let me;
it's who's going to stop me."
– Ayn Rand

I've been doing a lot of thinking lately about my life and if I am really living the way God intended me to live. Am I seeing things the way He would want me to see them, or am I letting regret and disappointment fill my thoughts throughout the day? Am I thinking about every mistake I have made, or have I learned from those mistakes? Am I pressing on with the goal of doing better in the future?

I decided that I'm not going to wait until I meet that perfect person or have enough money or whatever limitation I put on myself to live life to the fullest. That doesn't mean a reckless life of partying or crazy wild nights drinking until the sun comes up. For me, that means making a bucket list. I don't need to be sick or dying of a fatal disease to make a bucket list. Why should I wait to live until I am dying? Joyce Meyer once spoke about buying the shoes and eating the cookie if she wanted too. I like the way she thinks.

I think goals are achieved more often when we get them out of our imaginations and onto paper.

I'm tired of wishing my life away. So who wants to join me in creating their own bucket list?

A bucket list doesn't have to be composed of expensive or daring things. It could include something as simple as being on the beach when the sun rises or spending one whole day in bed reading a book.

Write it down and commit to doing it. Live your life intentionally. Don't let life just take you where it wants to, like waves on the ocean. Get in the boat and direct it to where you want to go!

Here are a few of mine:

1. Get a passport. (I never know when I might have an opportunity to go.)
2. Get a silver convertible. (I'm tired of the "mom" cars.)
3. Spend a month in Tuscany.
4. Go to the beach at least once this summer.

These are just a few things I am determined to do. If I fail at anything on my list, I will move onto the next thing until I can come back and try it again. Failing is not an option. I already picked up my application for my passport and made an appointment to have it processed. It just took little tiny steps to make that happen, but I am so excited that I am close to checking off one of my goals from the list already.

Grab your bucket and come take a ride with me in my silver convertible. It's going to be a good time.

The Perfect Storm

When I was a little girl growing up in Nebraska, tornadoes were somewhat commonplace during certain times of the year. I remember there were times when you could just feel one was about to happen. The sky would cast an antique orange color on all of the trees and houses. It reminded me of the sepia setting on an old 35 mm camera.

The birds became eerily silent, and a sweet smell infused the air. One morning I awoke to the sound of wind thrashing against the windows. In a sense of wonder, I meandered outside in my pajamas to see what was happening. Rain was blowing so hard that it felt like shards of glass were hitting my face. The funnel was so large it was all I could see. It seemed to fill the whole sky. It was swirling in my grandmother's back yard, and it was coming right toward me. Everything went white, and the sound of the funnel swirling was so loud. Everything it touched fell apart and was thrown into the air into little pieces.

Fear struck me and I called out for my mother to come save me, but when I looked behind me, I saw her look at me then she coldly turned away and ran off into the distance.

I cried out again, and in the midst of the storm and destruction, I could see grandmother's face coming towards me. But she wasn't running, she was walking calmly towards me. She appeared fearless with her arms outstretched. A feeling of peace came over me when everything else was falling apart. She reached me and put her arms around me and sheltered me with her body and almost immediately the storm vanished.

I then, of course, woke up because it was nightmare that I had been having! (Gotcha.) I have thought of that dream many times as an adult and wondered what God may have been trying to tell me. I think He was trying to tell me that even in the storms of our lives, He remains calm. He remains our protector. Even though I never felt like my mother wanted me or loved me, He did.

Even when I feel alone and that I have no one to save me, He already has.

About the Author

Dori Grassau is newly married to her first love. They reconnected after thirty years and now reside in North Carolina with her children and new grandchild.

For more encouragement and to purchase
additional copies of her book, follow Dori
on her blog at dorigrassau.com